# Empowering the Leader Within

*Virtus Press Publications*
127 Edgewood Avenue
Baltimore, Maryland 21228

First Virtus Press Edition 1995

Formative Leadership,Virtue-Quest,Virtue-Reality Square,Virtue-Reality Check, Virtue-Reality Wheel, Virtue Quotient, Virtue-P.A.C.T., and Virtue-Reality Network are all trademarks of The Center for Formative Leadership.

Library of Congress Catalog Card Number 95-90765

ISBN 0-9648722-0-X

Edited by Carol Wilcox.

Illustrations by Carmine.

Cover design by James M. Faulkner.

Printed in the United States of America.

To the Brocato and De Simone families:

--eight wonderful children--
--nine special grandchildren--


*Silver and gold I have none;*
*but what I have, I give you.*

[Acts 3:6]

Special Assistant to the Secretary, Maryland Department of Health and Mental Hygiene, who contributed a public sector perspective and shared the basic idea of "The Leadership Square" which we developed into the **Virtue-Reality Square**™; Peter B. Petersen, D.B.A., Professor of Management and Organization Theory, Division of Business and Management, School of Continuing Studies, Johns Hopkins University, who provided insightful comments on the necessity of emphasizing interpersonal human relationships in terms of the virtues; Kenneth A. Potocki, Ph.D., Assistant to the Director for Improvement, Applied Physics Laboratory, Johns Hopkins University, whose thorough and careful analysis helped us to keep the continuity of concepts throughout; Carol Wuenschel, Human Resources Director, Bank of Hanover, who supported us in the utilization of the adult experiential learning cycle as a framework for the presentation of this material; and to our families, friends, and colleagues without whose constant support this book would not have been finished.

# CONTENTS

# Leadership development is a life-time journey --not a brief trip.

**--John Maxwell[1]--**

# Introduction

This book is for anyone who directs, or aspires to direct, the activities of others. Whether you are a business owner, executive, administrator, manager, supervisor, or a family head to accomplish your mission you must be able to effectively lead others. The success of the unit you lead depends on how well you prepare yourself to do this.

If you were given a special set of "golden" keys and told that by simply opening four locked repositories you would be ensured the power to <u>achieve peak performance in leading others</u>, would you use those keys? Undoubtedly you would.

And if you knew that by opening those repositories you could acquire or **form** the habits to enable you to use this power wisely in any situation (at work or home or in society), you probably would not delay an instant. Those often missed keys which are essential for achieving peak leadership performance will be revealed within these pages.

Prepare to learn how leaders are really formed from the "inside-out." Prepare to use those four "golden" keys to discover the forgotten wisdom of an ancient cultural heritage--namely, our own. It is our sincere hope that you will let this book serve as a guide to facilitate your journey to **Formative Leadership**--empowering the leader within yourself.

"there is substantial evidence that leaders can significantly influence the performance and survival of complex organizations," a necessity in this new global environment in which we find ourselves.[5]

Bennis has said, "Failing organizations are usually over-managed and under-led."[6] The reverse of this situation is also often true. The following case illustrates this point.

An example of how good leadership can have a powerful impact on organizational performance is the Hewlett-Packard (HP) high-tech company located in Silicon Valley, California. HP was started in 1939 with a $538 seed investment, grew to $30 million in 1958 and by the end of fiscal 1994 sales topped $25 billion. It employs almost 99,000 people worldwide.

David Packard, in an interview discussing his new book *The HP Way*, focused on the values both he and co-founder William Hewlett fostered at Hewlett-Packard. "You've got to have leadership, you've got to know what you're doing, and you've got to play it straight," Mr. Packard said. Mr. Hewlett averred, "You've got to have concern for what your people do."[7]

Both leaders had great respect for their employees and were dedicated to a multitude of humanitarian causes, donating millions of dollars to education, the environment, and science. The success of the Hewlett-Packard company is greatly attributable to the qualities exhibited by the co-founders: leadership (vision and others decision-making), competency (knowing what you are doing), ethics (playing it straight), and character (concern for and dedication to causes larger than yourself). They are uncommonly effective leaders.

Our experience shows, that in spite of all the written material, training, and success stories such as Hewlett-Packard, we still have a lack of effective leaders. J. William Pfeiffer, in *Theories and Models in Applied Behavioral Science*, reported:

> Historian and political scientist James MacGregor Burns (1978) believes that leadership is one of the most studied and least understood elements of human interaction. Burns maintains that although over 130 definitions of leadership exist, considerably more is known about *leaders* than about *leadership*. As yet, society has not been able to grasp the essence of leadership and, as a result, is experiencing a serious "crisis of leadership" brought about by <u>mediocre</u> and <u>irresponsible</u> leaders (p. 215).[8]

Why are we still having a "crisis of leadership?" Why do we still have "mediocre" and "irresponsible" leaders? Empirical research provides us with some clues.

17

*If I try to use manipulative strategies and tactics to get other people to do what I want --while my character is flawed or my competency is questionable --then I can't be successful over time . . . . But if we learn to manage things and lead people, we will have the best bottom line because we will unleash the energy and talent of people.*

--Stephen R. Covey[12]--

According to Landy and Trumbo in *Psychology of Work Behavior*, motivation is related to some <u>innate characteristic</u> of individuals which require them to seek challenge, stimulation, and autonomy.[13] Motivation is intrinsic ("inside-out") to the individual and based on personal freedom.

Consequently, trying to influence others through the power of your own will or the power of your position, is nothing more than the "cult of the personality." It may work slightly in the short term, but never over the long haul.

Some researchers (Bass, 1991; Block, 1987; Burns, 1978; Maslow, 1970) claim that to motivate and lead others effectively requires "transformational leadership."[14] This inspirational type of leader is seen more as a "visionary," or one who promotes mutual stimulation and elevation through the satisfaction of what Maslow described as "higher-order" needs (e. g., "belonging," "esteem," and "self-actualization").

The transformational leader focuses on follower <u>empowerment</u> and involvement as the "ends" envisioned as opposed to personal positional power as a "means" to goal attainment. For a transformational leader, power <u>comes from within</u> and is distributive. Transformational leaders are evaluated by: 1) their impact on the human condition, 2) equality and justice, and 3) the extent to which they facilitate or inhibit standards of good conduct.[15]

# Formative Leadership
## --A Philosophical Framework

Stephen R. Covey, in *The 7 Habits of Highly Effective People,* may have articulated it best when he stated that we must make a paradigm shift away from the personality ethic. What we need is to help build "deep integrity and fundamental <u>character</u>" in each individual.[17]

We agree with Dr. Covey. We also believe this shift demands that we rediscover a new philosophical framework which we call **Formative Leadership**; the "inside-out" process of "shaping" or "molding" those interior character qualities ("being" comes first) necessary for the effective leadership and motivation of others ("action" follows). Your personality and reputation precede you. They are what other people see and think you are. "Character" (your nature, constitution, or makeup), however, is what you really are deep <u>inside</u>. **Action follows being; character does matter![18]**

The word "character" comes to us from a Greek verb which means making a furrow, cutting a groove, or putting a scratch on something as a mark. In the light of its origin, we may think of character as that which puts its mark on a human being. Character is what makes you what you are as distinct from other persons. The individual is little more than a "bundle of feelings" unless there is some central loyalty within creating order out of the "chaos of the soul." Character signifies the organization of life and behavior

24

around a central loyalty which has ethical worth and validity. Character in this sense is more than a sum of personality traits. It is in fact a "clustering of personal qualities" around some major article of personal conviction.

Our strength of character, then, is derived from some organizing principle in life, a major purpose we cherish. Character is strong where this central loyalty is powerful enough to produce order in the experiences of life. Character is weak, on the other hand, where no such central persuasion exists, or when it is a weak principle that has no organizing force.

Character is something dynamic. It moves in certain directions. Character is the internal **power** with which we behave in response to the prompting of conscience. The strengthening of character is primarily a matter of not only knowing one's self but of putting to work the principle, "Master thyself!"

The leader's character is not **formed** without effort. Every action either develops or degrades character. Good deeds (virtues) leave their effects, and so do the bad ones (vices). Self-discipline is chiefly a matter of **choosing the good deeds for the effect they have on what I am** and of avoiding the bad ones for the harm they can do to my character. In the matter of **Formative Leadership** as it relates to character, there is such a thing as self-sacrifice, "losing one's life to find it." In fact, some of the outstanding characters of world history have been people who devoted their time and energies to some larger cause outside themselves.

*What Is Virtue?*
*You can't lose it,*
*like virginity, and*
*don't confuse it with*
*'values,' which vary.*
*Throughout a long,*
*rich history, it's meant*
*doing the right thing.*

--NEWSWEEK (1994)21--

# Formative Leadership & Virtue
## --The Missing Link

Formative <u>Leadership</u> is inexorably linked to <u>character</u> which is linked to <u>personal power</u>. To not possess one is to not possess the others. A leader is indeed a powerful person as well as a powerful force.

How is all this linked to the quaint, almost archaic sounding concept known as **virtue**? By definition, <u>personal virtue is personal power</u>. Virtue comes to us from the Latin **virtus** which in esssence means **power**.

Dr. David Isaacs stated, in *Character Building*, there are "a whole series of <u>virtues</u> which help a person to have more self-mastery so [they] can better serve, contribute to, others."[22] These human virtues, we maintain, are the "golden" keys--the <u>character builders</u>--needed to ensure the <u>personal power</u> to achieve peak leadership performance.

Human virtue is a proactive quality, a definite tendency which predisposes someone to action in accordance with ethical judgement, and can be acquired by developing the <u>habit</u> of suitable acts (behavior). To be virtuous one must act virtuously.

*Correct principles
are like compasses:
they are always
pointing the way.
And if we know how
to read them, we won't
get lost, confused,
or fooled by conflicting
voices and values.*

**--Stephen R. Covey[23]--**

# Discovering the Power of Formative Leadership --Four "Golden" Keys

There are four "golden" keys to **Formative Leadership** which are necessary to truly empower a person to develop the leader's personal power from within. They are based on ethical[1] principles or rules of life which help us to **respect the other person and to work together with others** in the performance

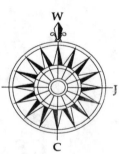

of our daily tasks. These four keys are not only universal human virtues in their own right, but also types or main categories of subsidiary virtues. The ancient Greek sages knew them as <u>Prudence</u>, <u>Fortitude</u>, <u>Justice</u>, and <u>Temperance</u>; in the modern vernacular we know them as Wisdom, Courage, Justice, and Inner-Order[24]:

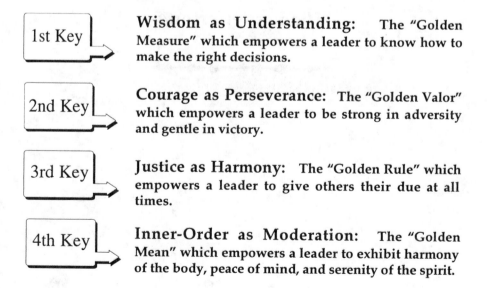

**1st Key** → **Wisdom as Understanding:** The "Golden Measure" which empowers a leader to know how to make the right decisions.

**2nd Key** → **Courage as Perseverance:** The "Golden Valor" which empowers a leader to be strong in adversity and gentle in victory.

**3rd Key** → **Justice as Harmony:** The "Golden Rule" which empowers a leader to give others their due at all times.

**4th Key** → **Inner-Order as Moderation:** The "Golden Mean" which empowers a leader to exhibit harmony of the body, peace of mind, and serenity of the spirit.

*And if the Wise
be the happy man,
as these sages say,
he must be virtuous too;
for without virtue
happiness cannot be.*

**--Thomas Jefferson[25]--**

These four keys are also known as the "four hinges on which swing the gates of life." They come down to us as the **Four Cardinal Virtues** (from the Latin word "cardo" or "hinge"); four essential virtues to which the characteristics of empowered leaders may be traced.

The Greeks (Plato, Aristotle) and Romans (Cicero, Seneca) knew them; so did both Judaism (Philo) and Christianity (Augustine of Hippo). Philosophers believe this specific rational framework was one of the great discoveries in the history of humankind's self-understanding.

The accumulated literature of the ages--across all cultures--is replete with the great sagas of virtuous leaders. There we see leaders who help others to overcome adversity and achieve personal excellence through the practice of the virtues. There we see leaders who lead with that "illumination of moral existence," which, as stated in one of the wisest books of the East, is denied any person who looks only at himself or herself. Lao-Tzu in *Tao Te Ching* said, "He who looks at himself does not shine."[26]

Empowering the leader within, or **Formative Leadership** as we call it, is an "inside-out" approach. From within, from the center of being, flows the source of a person's operational principles. We work best to achieve peak leadership performance from the "inside-out."

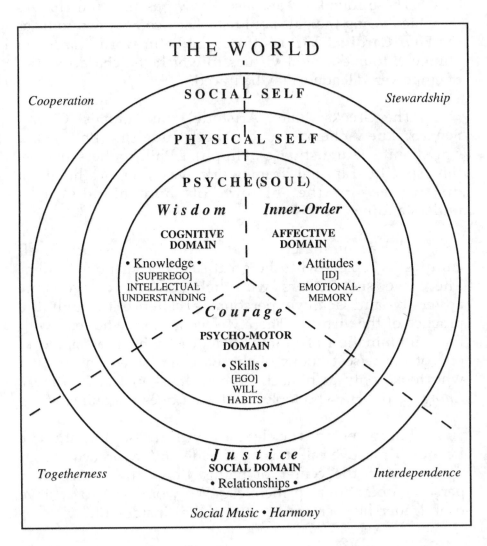

THE WORLD

*Cooperation*          SOCIAL SELF          *Stewardship*

PHYSICAL SELF

PSYCHE(SOUL)

*Wisdom*     |     *Inner-Order*

COGNITIVE DOMAIN     AFFECTIVE DOMAIN

• Knowledge •          • Attitudes •
[SUPEREGO]               [ID]
INTELLECTUAL           EMOTIONAL-
UNDERSTANDING          MEMORY

*Courage*

PSYCHO-MOTOR DOMAIN

• Skills •
[EGO]
WILL
HABITS

*Justice*
SOCIAL DOMAIN
• Relationships •

*Togetherness*                    *Interdependence*

*Social Music • Harmony*

A Model for Formative Leadership

Habits can be "good" (virtues)--appropriate, effective, efficient, moral, etc., or habits can be "bad" (vices)--inappropriate, ineffective, wasteful, immoral, etc. Forming good habits by practicing the four essential virtues and their various subsidiary virtues, particularly those pertinent to leadership, will empower the leader from within.

The model on the facing page depicts the leader who has been "empowered" from within (by practicing the habits of the key virtues) relative to others and the "World." Each essential virtue has been linked to various other conceptual frameworks (e. g. the cognitive, affective, psycho-motor, and social domains; knowledge, attitudes, skills, relationships, etc.).

This model helps to explain the connection of the different parts of the self to each other as well as to interactions with other individuals. Note that Wisdom, Inner-Order and Courage show a locus within the psyche (Greek for soul). Justice emanates from the psyche when all three other virtues are in place. Justice is shown in the ring of the "social self" where it is actualized as relationships--interdependence, "social music," or being in harmony with others.

Applying this "inside-out" model as a process-in-action enables the leader to achieve peak leadership performance. The model is new, but the concepts are time-tested and true.[27] Many leaders of note have trusted these principles.

Frank Bettger, in *How I Raised Myself From Failure to Success. . .*, and Harry Roberts and Bernard Sergesketter, in *Quality is Personal*,[28] gave an example of a type of process which embodies the principles of what we call **Formative Leadership**. The leader they described was Benjamin Franklin. Even though Franklin admittedly had many faults, he did recognize, however, the fact that he should improve himself through the formation of his character.

Franklin thought of himself as a simple man of ordinary ability. He had two years of formal education. He also believed that he could acquire the habits necessary to develop a successful life. So, he invented a practical plan of action for improvement. The method is described in *The Autobiography of Benjamin Franklin*.

Franklin chose 13 characteristics he thought desirable to acquire or master. Then he gave each point, in turn, rigorous attention for one week. This simple method enabled him to go through the whole list in 13 weeks, repeating the process four times in a year.

Franklin believed to this one method he owed his success and all that he did that was good. What was on old Ben Franklin's "self-improvement" list? You may be surprised to learn that the following list, given as he originally wrote them in his autobiography, consisted mainly of the human virtues.

1. <u>Temperance</u>--Eat not to dullness; drink not to elevation.

2. <u>Silence</u>--Speak not but what may benefit others or yourself; avoid trifling conversation.

3. <u>Order</u>--Let all your things have their places; let each part of your business have its time.

4. <u>Resolution</u>--Resolve to perform what you ought; perform without fail what you resolve.

5. <u>Frugality</u>--Make no expense but to do good to others or yourself; i.e., waste nothing.

6. <u>Industry</u>--Lose no time; be always employed in something useful; cut off all unnecessary actions.

7. <u>Sincerity</u>--Use no hurtful deceit; think innocently and justly, and, if you speak, speak accordingly.

8. <u>Justice</u>--Wrong none by doing injuries, or omitting the benefits that are your duty.

9. <u>Moderation</u>--Avoid extremes; forbear resenting injuries so much as you think they deserve.

10. <u>Cleanliness</u>--Tolerate no uncleanliness in body, cloaths, or habitation.

11. <u>Tranquility</u>--Be not disturbed at trifles, or at accidents common or unavoidable.

12. <u>Chastity</u>--Rarely use venery but for health or offspring, never to dullness, weakness, or the injury of your own or another's peace or reputation.

13. <u>Humility</u>--Imitate Jesus and Socrates.

*We are what we
repeatedly do;
excellence then
is not an act,
but a habit.*

**--Aristotle[29]--**

Of this experiment Franklin wrote, "I was surprised to find myself so much fuller of faults than I imagined; but I had the satisfaction of seeing them diminish." He continued to keep score on himself off and on almost his entire life. In this way Benjamin Franklin used the idea of a checklist to improve his ethical character. He saw clearly that what we do, and fail to do, plays a great part in making us what we are today and will be tomorrow.

Somewhere along the line we have lost sight of what really makes an uncommonly effective leader--the personal habit of virtuous behavior, the strength of character, which comes from within. Behavior which inspires others to do the same through example; behavior which <u>empowers others to share in that leadership</u>.

The remainder of this book will examine each of these four essential keys to **Formative Leadership** in depth. We will attempt to explain why and how each should be acquired. We will give examples of each key in action. And, we will provide action steps and suggest proven methods by which you may develop your character in order to empower the leader within and achieve peak leadership performance.

# PART TWO: THE PRINCIPLES

*Self-discipline, compassion, responsibility, work, friendship, perseverance, honesty, loyalty. . . . They're not just nice ideas, they're the foundation for truly productive and profitable business relationships. And how clearly your organization reflects those virtues has a direct affect on its ability to inspire, unite and lead its workforce.*

**--William Bennett[30]--**

# Introduction to the Principles

As we have already seen, the chief function of **Formative Leadership** is to empower the leader within. This is accomplished by the formation of character through the practice of virtuous habits, many of which hinge on the four Cardinal Virtues.

A virtue is positive energy which is proactive in life, "molding" or "shaping" patterns of individual behavior, thereby forming character. In this part, the principle tenets of these four keys and their subsidiary virtues pertinent to the formation of leaders will be considered and presented according to the following conceptual framework (see **A Model for Formative Leadership,** p. 36).

**ARRANGEMENT OF VIRTUES
ACCORDING TO THE MODEL OF FORMATIVE LEADERSHIP**

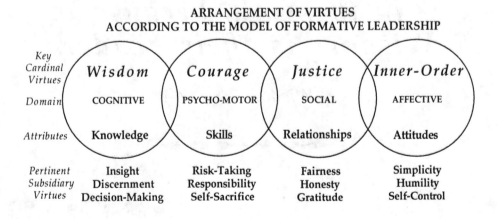

| |  |  |  |  |
|---|---|---|---|---|
| *Key Cardinal Virtues* | *Wisdom* | *Courage* | *Justice* | *Inner-Order* |
| *Domain* | COGNITIVE | PSYCHO-MOTOR | SOCIAL | AFFECTIVE |
| *Attributes* | Knowledge | Skills | Relationships | Attitudes |
| *Pertinent Subsidiary Virtues* | Insight Discernment Decision-Making | Risk-Taking Responsibility Self-Sacrifice | Fairness Honesty Gratitude | Simplicity Humility Self-Control |

*All good things
together came to me
in her company,
and countless riches
at her hands;
and I rejoiced
in them all, because
Wisdom is their Leader.*

*--Wisdom 7:11-12--*

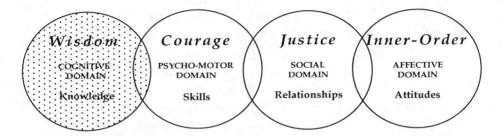

*1st Key: Wisdom as Understanding is the Golden Measure which empowers a leader to make the right decisions.*

# Tenets of Wisdom

**Wisdom as Understanding** (or Prudence) ". . . is not cautious calculation but <u>practical wisdom</u>--recognizing and making the right choice in specific situations. It is the master virtue that makes all others possible."[31]  It is, therefore, the "mother" or source of all virtues; the **Golden Measure** of Justice, of Courage, of Inner-Order. It is the intellectual virtue of adapting one's behavior in accordance with objective standards based on ethical grounds. It is the attribute which enables a leader to make <u>good use</u> of knowledge, judgment, sagacity, and similar powers.

One who exercises practical wisdom (or prudence), perceives the truth of real things, so that conformity of mind to reality itself may guide him or her to the proper means for realizing his or her goal. <u>The practice of this key virtue allows a leader to correctly discern not only what to do, but to choose the best possible alternatives among several choices.</u> It deals with the habit of taking things into consideration and weighing their importance in a given situation.

It is well to remember that the word "conscience" is intimately related to the word "prudence."  <u>It prompts the will, or volition of the leader to act virtuously</u>.  It implies a sound memory of past experiences and proper understanding of the present situation.  It is the habit of moral discernment which indicates to the leader's will how to respond in accordance with, or operationalize, all other virtues.

To empower the leader within, it is essential to master three subsidiaries of practical wisdom (or prudence): <u>insight</u>, <u>discernment</u>, and <u>decision-making</u>.  Insight is that ability which enables a leader to size up any situation with an intuitive "third eye;" the penetrating mental vision of seeing into inner character or underlying truth; also, the ability to see yourself as others see you--self-knowledge.

Discernment, the second subsidiary, is acuteness of judgement; the ability of a leader to evaluate facts or opinions in light of qualitative standards.  The third subsidiary, decision-making, is that process of making up your mind or determining a course of action based on sound premises.  It necessitates that the leader seek counsel or advice from those above or below them before making a final decision.  Decision-making also encompasses an aspect of prudence which is the habit of judging all actions in relation to the final goal of life; ". . . keep the end in view, follow nature" (Lucan, 39-65 A. D.).

*It is by the goodness
of God that in our country
we have those three
unspeakably precious
things: freedom of speech,
freedom of conscience, and
the <u>prudence</u> never to
practice either of them.*

**--Mark Twain (Samuel Langhorne Clemens)--**

# Reflections on Wisdom

Wisdom (or prudence) is that quality which directs a leader's decisions, desires and actions toward an identified goal. Its practice positions, as it were, landmarks on your internal field of vision; giving direction and destination to your goals.

This practical wisdom encompasses memory and desire, intellect or insight, as well as truth and consequences. It depends on your ability to remember what past experience has taught, know the entire reality of the present circumstance, and accurately weigh the future consequences of all possible considerations--and then to "do the <u>right thing</u>"--a definition of quality leadership![32]

Capable leaders practice this virtue at all intuitive moments of decision; and learn from their mistakes. We "know" when an action or decision does NOT "feel prudent," just as President John F. Kennedy discovered during the Bay of Pigs fiasco. We also "know" when it does, as the world witnessed when President Kennedy subsequently responded to the Cuban Missile Crisis. The sensitivity of prudence resonates with an inner calm about the truth of our perceptions reflected in our decisions, which may have great impact on our world. Peace of mind about our decisions, free from anxiety and inner questioning, is a universal desire of all leaders.

And when do we act with practical wisdom? When we think before we act; when we act <u>with others in mind</u>; when we sacrifice individual desires for the common good. Superior managers practice this key virtue when they make decisions taking into account their employees' circumstances. All leaders use practical wisdom when they weigh both the alternatives and consequences when making personal and professional decisions.

The distinguishing feature of this virtue is the depth of the field of vision that it encompasses. Practical wisdom (or prudence) acts as the "Golden Measure" by which we are able to practice the other virtues of Justice, Courage, and Inner-Order. It allows us to view the entire situation relative to the particular circumstances of the individual; to consider the "big picture." Discerning, judging, weighing alternatives, thoughtfully deciding, and finally acting with the goal in mind is another way to perceive this practical wisdom.

Through the acquisition of and practice of this virtue, leaders are able to properly see the details of their daily lives and duties impacted against the larger background of their vision of the future. It is against this "impact of the larger background" that great leaders are able to make "discerning" decisions.

Decisions define dreams. They put boundaries around who we are and what we stand for. They are a way of connecting with life's circumstances, challenging our patterns of interacting with others. Decisions can be emotional, well-thought out, weighed, prolonged, responsible, passionate, judgmental, etc. There are endless adjectives to describe the many parts of ourselves involved in the decision-making process. Many of these adjectives may be simultaneously operative when weighing the consequences of a decision. Why? Because it asks us to view our leadership as truly unique; an integral part of the greater scheme of things, for the greater good. It asks us to search for the best solution, and once found, command the will to act on the decision with insight and discernment.

Practical wisdom as we have discovered, is essential to achieving peak leadership performance, because it is the foundation of the leader's competency in using all the resources available to formulate goals and actions to insure the right outcome. It is also the cornerstone upon which rests the ability to practice Justice, Courage, and Inner-Order since these virtues also involve discernment of concepts such as truth, rightness, and lastingness. Understood in this sense, **Formative Leadership** itself is the empowerment of all the Cardinal Virtues for discovering truth, rightness, and lastingness while engaged in conducting business as usual.

The practical wisdom inherent in **Formative Leadership** then becomes the window through which one witnesses the transfer of empowerment to others. It is not only the vision of where we, as leaders can be; it is the vision of where we, as leaders, must be. For the leader, this key virtue is the ability to animate, propel and project their inner-vision of the future into the here and now through appropriate decisions and action which reflect the truth, rightness, and lastingness of that vision to others.

Seeing with the inner-eye (prudently), through the lens of practical wisdom, leaders simultaneously see with foresight, hindsight, and peripheral vision. As leaders, our decision-making is based on our inner and outer eyes and determines the ultimate destination of those visions.

Wisdom as Understanding is the most uplifting of all the virtues. It allows us to constantly recall, re-create, and rejoice in our day-to-day perceptions, insights, and decisions which <u>impact our interactions with others</u>.

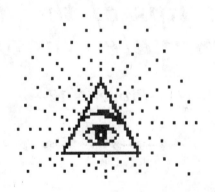

*Prudence is the eye of the soul. Without eyes we cannot see the way to go.*

**--Aquinas--**

53

# The mind of the intelligent . . .seeks knowledge. . . the lips of the wise disseminate knowledge.

*--Proverbs 15--*

## Exercises in Wisdom:
### Knowledge/Attitudes/Skills/Relationships

1. Get a book of "insightful sayings" for leaders (e. g., Stephen Covey's *Principled Centered Leadership*, James Kouzes and Barry Posner's *The Leadership Challenge*, etc.)[33] and keep a journal in which you record "notable quotes" from your reading which help you to "see yourself as others see you." Jot down in your calendar one of these quotes which could serve as a "reflection" on "self-knowledge" for the week. Review it frequently during the day. Pick a new one every week!

2. "Discernment" is keen judgement. Give yourself an "attitude check" the next time you need to make an important choice. Weigh your choice against your positive vision of the future and the impact on others to see if there is clear alignment. Keep in mind what Emerson said, "The thought is the ancestor of the deed."

3. Identify at least three specific "competencies" (purposeful and productive behaviors) you need to work on which will help you improve your "decision-making" (e. g., problem-solving, strategic planning, process improvement, team building, etc.). Seek further skill building in one of those areas now. Plan to gain skill in the other areas in the near future.

*Courage is that perfection
which keeps a person firm
in the presence of fear.
It demands patience
and constancy
and often heroism.*

--Martin Harrison (1947)--

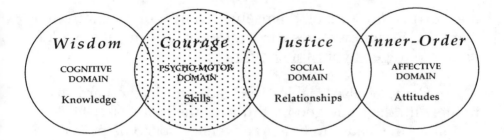

*2nd Key : Courage as Perseverance is the Golden Valor which empowers a leader to be strong in adversity and gentle in victory.*

# Tenets of Courage

**Courage as Perseverance** could be best described as the **Golden Valor** of our heart. Courage is also known as Fortitude, which means "strength of soul." This second, of the four essential virtues, empowers the leader within to adhere to the good and noble through all trials and tribulations, regardless of "public opinion," even to the very end. It is the determination to see things through all adversity.

Leaders need all the courage necessary to face the many difficulties and hardships which life brings to each one of us. When the going gets tough, there is a tendency in human nature to take the path of least resistance; underestimating the importance of, or the consequences of, our actions. Courage empowers a leader to face those people, places, or circumstances which he or she most fears while resisting reckless or irresponsible behavior. Our fears are not bad in and of themselves, only our uncontrolled fears. Courage involves the control of, not the absence of, fear. <u>Courage is your inner strength</u>!

Courage also enables the leader to do the hard tasks in life with the same good attitude as the easy tasks. It does not allow the leader to bow to adversity nor to be puffed up by prosperity. Courage shows no excessive pride in success nor despair in failure. It combines in itself such qualities as strength, vigor, endurance, and self-sacrifice. This virtue is the support of all other virtues.

Courage is also a category of related virtues which includes <u>risk-taking</u>, <u>responsibility</u>, and <u>self-sacrifice</u>; key subsidiary virtues for anyone desiring to achieve peak leadership performance. The first, risk-taking, is the willingness to take chances by getting out of your comfort zone. To dare to be different. And, at the same time using common sense to abandon a course of action when it is right to do so.

Responsibility, the second subsidiary, is accepting the effect of your leadership actions, intended or unintended (resulting from decision-making), so that <u>others either benefit as much as possible</u> or, at least, do not suffer the consequences. The third key subsidiary virtue of courage as perseverance is self-sacrifice. This is the willingness to go beyond the call of duty or to walk the extra mile. It is manifested in leaders as stewardship; <u>always being quick to help others, and loving to do so</u>, amenable to taking second place and letting someone else be the "star." Self-sacrifice empowers the servant-leader within.

*You gain strength,*
*courage, and confidence*
*by every experience*
*in which you really stop*
*to look fear in the face.*
*You are able to say to yourself,*
*"I lived through this horror.*
*I can take the next thing*
*that comes along."*
*. . .You must do the thing*
*you think you cannot do.*

**--Eleanor Roosevelt (1960)--**

# Reflections on Courage

Courage (or fortitude) is the integration of the body, mind, emotional, psychological, and spiritual aspects of the individual which make it possible for one to sustain oneself and lead others even under the most adverse circumstances. Courage is the second virtue in the developmental process of acquiring the four Cardinal Virtues because it empowers the leader's inner strength which is necessary to operationalize the other virtues. It is our "Golden Valor!"

"My strength is the strength of ten, because my heart is pure,"said Sir Galahad (Alfred, Lord Tennyson, 1842). In medieval times, knights would endure years of training and physical conditioning culminating in rituals of fasting and prayer, making it possible for them to achieve the actual "knighting" ceremony: an outward sign of their unfailing and proven inner fortitude. Even now, we use the word "courageous" in our language to express that aspect of sustaining willpower to strengthen, endure, or secure oneself against any attack on our person, our possessions, or our integrity.

However, another dimension of courage in our daily lives is exemplified in our personal commitment to excellence. Are we as leaders committed to our own spirituality, spouses, children, families, work, professional endeavors, personal promises, and positive visions of the future? Are we committed to improving daily our efforts in these endeavors?

Commitment means a turning of our will toward our vision of the future, and setting goals to guide our journey. It is a journey, however, that does, in fact, require resolute courage at times.

It has been said that a Northern minister once remarked to the late Dr. Martin Luther King, Jr. that he was "involved" in the civil rights movement. Dr. King responded with, "that's nice that you are involved, but are you committed?" "Involvement, commitment, what's the difference?" averred the minister. "Commitment," said Dr. King, "is like a ham and eggs breakfast--the chicken is INVOLVED, but the pig is COMMITTED!"

Leadership requires the courage to make sacrifices, deflect distractions, stay on course, realize the worth of our goal, and stay focused on the vision and to show others the way by our example. It takes preparation or planning and right-behavior to reflect the internal destination, the desire of our heart.

We understand desire as the inner motivation, the inspiration, the internal spark which ignites the practice of courage. Yes, it takes guts, it takes courage, to withstand the demands on our time, the temptations of infidelity to our visions, and the arduous trails to goal attainment.

Daily we fortify our visions by doing those small acts of the will which further our aspirations and refuel our desire. As the ancient Chinese Proverb says: "A journey of a thousand miles begins with but a single step."

The practice of courage is a continuously developing interplay of mind, body, and spirit working in harmony with the will to realize the inner vision. It is the development of the will which ultimately matures all three elements of mind, body, and spirit which constitute the whole self.

And who are the empowered leaders, the heroes and heroines of courage in action? All those who honor commitments: marital, professional, personal, emotional, academic, spiritual, and/or temporal. Those who do not see walking away from a problem as an acceptable solution. Those who are willing to stand up for their beliefs.

The soldier willing to serve. The leader willing to LEAD with conviction. Those who comfort in times of distress. Those who rescue in times of crisis. Those who teach in much less than favorable learning environments. Those who heal the hurts and wounds of physical and/or emotional injury. Those who nurse the sick, especially the terminally ill. Those who raise children, natural, adopted, fostered, differently-abled, troubled, or just plain kids. Those who shelter the homeless, share with the unfortunate, serve the needy.

Empowered, also, are those who continue to hope for a better tomorrow based on their personal actions to begin to achieve their vision today. Those who "light a candle" rather than "curse the darkness." We are practitioners of courage in every action, re-action, and interaction in which we fully participate, uniting our wills, aligning our minds, and strengthening the spirit of commitment toward the attainment of that virtue.

Courage as Perserverance is the virtue that is aligned with achievement. Like everything else that is worth while, it comes with hard work; for it is a frame of mind which does not let go, an attitude which gives us the power to accomplish a given task without allowing ourselves to be side-tracked by the difficulties that get in the way. Without it, there is no resolute purpose to our actions; with it we are unstoppable until our vision becomes a shared reality. Courage is the "right stuff" virtue, the lineage of true leaders.

*It is better to light a candle than to curse the darkness.*

*--Chinese Proverb--*

*Press On!*
*Nothing in the World*
*can take the place of*
*PERSISTENCE!*
*Talent will not;*
*nothing is more common*
*than unsuccessful*
*men with talent.*
*Genius will not;*
*unrewarded genius*
*is almost a proverb.*
*Education will not;*
*the world is full of*
*educated derelicts.*
*PERSISTENCE and*
*DETERMINATION*
*alone are omnipotent!*

--Calvin Coolige (1872-1933)--

# Exercises in Courage:
## Knowledge/Attitudes/Skills/Relationships

1. Visit your local library or bookstore and get a book on a courageous personage from history (e. g., John F. Kennedy's *Profiles in Courage*, Helen Keller's *The Story of My Life*, etc.).[34]  Read it and select one virtue or quality you found admirable about the person.  How does that virtue apply to your own circumstances? For one week try to practice that virtue in your daily life; record in a journal personal learning from your effort.

2. Check your attitude concerning courage.  Spend some time TODAY reflecting on the many "courageous" acts performed daily by seemingly ordinary folks (i. e., fire fighters, paramedics, nurses, teachers, police, etc.).  Make a note to acknowledge the risks they take the next time you run across one of these individuals in the line of duty.  With the rise of violence in our society, we can no longer take courageous behavior for granted.

3. Develop "self-mastery" in courageous behavior, do two things today which you do not want to do,  yet need to be done, "just for exercise" of the will (e. g., "coach" a difficult employee, practice active listening with a spouse or significant other, etc.).  Keep a record of your daily progress in doing the hard, but right, thing.

# *Justice is that virtue of the soul which is distributive according to desert.*

## --Aristotle--

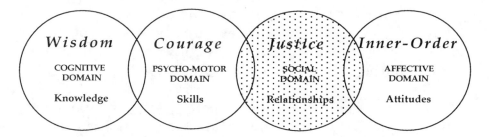

*3rd Key: Justice as Harmony is the Golden Rule which empowers a leader to give others their due at all times.*

# Tenets of Justice

**Justice as Harmony** is the key which enables a leader to render to others their due with perpetual and constant good will; the **Golden Rule** in action. It is an attitude of heart found in the minds of persons who are just. "What distinguishes justice from love is just this: in the relationship of Justice, [people] confront each other as separate 'others,' almost as strangers."[35] Justice is not concerned with self control, but rather with controlling our actions relative to another's possessions. The Just Leader does right by others not because of any relationship with them, but because it is the right thing to do; respecting another's "natural rights---life, liberty, and the pursuit of happiness."

By its extent, justice is one of the most far-reaching of the virtues. It <u>governs all of our relationships with others</u>. It is concerned with the right of each individual to their own existence and to those other possessions which they hold by right of natural law. It is concerned with the rights of society. <u>Justice aims at setting up a relationship of perfect equality between ourselves and others</u>.

67

By its very nature, justice includes the practice of many lesser virtues. It includes three pertinent subsidiary virtues which are important for empowering the leader within: <u>fairness</u>, <u>honesty</u>, and <u>gratitude</u>.

Fairness guides a leader to be <u>equitable</u> in all dealings with others. It soothes the exactitude of the process of Justice by applying the "gentle rain of mercy." The practice of fairness enables a leader to give others a chance by not always demanding the "pound of flesh." Fair leaders often exhibit an unprejudiced, even-handed, impartial way of dealing with others.

Honesty, the second subsidiary, is that faculty which deters a leader from taking or using anything that does not rightly belong to them. Don Shula and Ken Blanchard in *Everyone's A Coach* said, "Effective leaders are clear and straightforward in their interactions with others. Everything they do is HONESTY-BASED."[36] An honest leader is a person with moral fiber; a person of good character--manifested by their fidelity, integrity, and sincerity to sound principles. <u>Honesty begins in the heart</u>!

The third subsidiary, gratitude, is that quality known as reciprocity, meaning to give and take mutually. A leader practices this virtue by making appreciative reciprocation to his or her supporters, those who have assisted them. Gratitude is giving recognition for benefits received. It allows <u>another's efforts to be acknowledged</u> and allows others to see the individual as the leader perceives them!

*Justice is the first
of the virtues, for,
unsupported by justice,
valor is good for nothing;
and if all men were first,
there would be
no need of valor.*

--Agesilaus (Plutarch) --

# Reflections on Justice

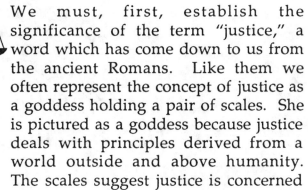

We must, first, establish the significance of the term "justice," a word which has come down to us from the ancient Romans. Like them we often represent the concept of justice as a goddess holding a pair of scales. She is pictured as a goddess because justice deals with principles derived from a world outside and above humanity. The scales suggest justice is concerned with weighing out for each person their proportionate share of rights and responsibilities. She wields a sword because it is her business to punish the person who disregards the balance among the rights of individuals and violates the rules of law and order in society. Her eyes are blindfolded to represent the impartial practice of justice. Some of the ancient rabbis called justice one of the "three pillars upholding the world," the other two being truth and peace.[37]

Justice involves the skilled practice, the art really, of <u>acknowledging the entire individual</u> and his or her particular circumstances, talents, abilities, and personal preferences in an equitable relationship, whether that relationship be professional or personal. To be able to discern the depth and breadth of the needed knowledge of those circumstances, in order to <u>honor the whole person,</u> calls for the finely tuned practice of justice as an <u>attitude of heart,</u> and a strength of **Formative Leadership**.

This same virtue also calls for the integration of the knowledge of those circumstances peculiar to the other person, together with the particular circumstances of the social action called for in each situation. Now we begin to understand why, within the haze of humanity, justice is indeed a beacon of light reflecting individual acknowledgement within the rights of society.

The habit of justice requires reflection and practice, the ability to see the situation as others see it, to be empathic, to listen to the individual with whom one is interacting, rather than simply treating others routinely. Justice is more than courtesy, more than common sense, more than respect. Justice implies an integration of the individual within a particular context, within a particular moment in time, acknowledging the many facets of the interaction.

Understood in this perspective, who is it then, who practices the virtue of justice? It is practiced by those who minister to the needs of others: economical, social, emotional, psychological, and/or physical in an attempt to minister to the whole person.

Leaders who recognize their personal biases and <u>do not allow themselves to discriminate</u> against any individual based on their race, color, gender, age, disability, or religious belief. All those who develop the permanent intention of <u>respecting the rights of others</u> keep the practice of justice alive.

We also serve justly as we lead through example: those who receive no payment for humanitarian services rendered; those who offer time, money, and/or materials in the service of others; those who listen, truly listen, before speaking or deciding.

Justice is not judgmental. In fact, its practice is quite the opposite. Justice is the deliberate utilization of one's resources and leadership in the service of another not because you "owe" them, but simply because they are "other" and it is their due. Mother Teresa, Albert Schweitzer, Tom Dooley, indeed, all the great humanitarians, practice the virtue of Justice in their pursuit of service to those in need. Working for and supporting organizations who directly impact the rights and dignity of the individual also allows us to exercise the pursuit of Justice.

It seems, however, that another aspect of this "beacon of light" embodied in the Just Leader is its ability to attract others to its practice. This aspect of justice is evident in the consistent practice by the leader of the "Golden Rule"--"Do unto others <u>as you would have them</u> do unto you."

Notice that the rule is not "She who has the Gold (money), makes the rules," nor the "military model"--"He who wears the Gold (insignias of office), rules." And, it is not "do it (evil) to others before they do it to you" or "do (good) unto others <u>if others do unto you</u>," or "do unto others <u>when they get around to doing</u> (good) unto you."

It would be easy to treat others justly if they treated us that way first. No, the operational assumption in the "Golden Rule" is that others <u>are not currently treating us justly</u>! Perhaps they are even treating us with great disdain and abuse.

We must visualize how we would want others to treat us in the future, not how they are actually treating us now! And then, we must lead the way first by our example and treat others <u>AS WE WOULD HAVE</u> (future tense) them treat us. Simple yes, easy no! No one has ever said that **Formative Leadership** would be easy.

*Leadership is not wielding authority --it's empowering\ people.*

--Becky Brodin[38]--

# Only the just man enjoys peace of mind.

**--Epicurus--**

# Exercises in Justice:
## Knowledge/Attitudes/Skills/Relationships

1. Read a section from a book (e. g., William Bennett's *Book of Virtues*)[39] which includes the Cardinal Virtue of justice, or one of its subsidiaries--fairness, honesty, or gratitude. Reflect on how you can apply the various aspects of justice to improve your leadership performance. Record your ideas in your journal and begin to apply them.

2. "Know thyself!" Reflect on your personal motives and behavior in dealing with others. Have you offended or harmed anyone by your behavior? If "yes," make amends in an appropriate manner, acknowledging the dignity of that individual.

3. Today, be pro-active about giving three people (e. g., superiors, subordinates, peers, etc.) their "due" (i. e., your respect, time, courtesy, best work efforts, etc.). Continue to give another three people their due tomorrow. Keep a record of how this practice improves your skills in relating to others.

*A thing moderately good
is not so good
as it ought to be.
Moderation in temper
is always a virtue; but
moderation in principle
is always a vice.*

**---Thomas Paine--**
*The Rights of Man*

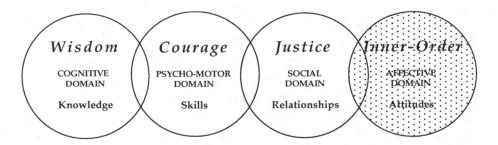

*4th Key: Inner-Order as Moderation is the Golden Mean*
*which empowers a leader to exhibit unity of life*
*--body, mind, and spirit.*

# Tenets of Inner-Order

**Inner-Order as Moderation** (or Temperance) is the key which empowers a leader to dispose the various parts of themselves in one unified whole--harmony of the body, peace of mind, and serenity of the spirit. It is the ability to understand what the Greeks referred to as the **Golden Mean** between excess and defect in the matter of the exercise of our behavior. Like the "temperate zone" lying between the "torrid" and "frigid" zones, Inner-Order as Moderation is the choice of the happy medium between too much and too little of anything.

Inner-Order is the virtue which keeps an individual's sensitive appetites in check, under the control of reason, so that they are not carried away by passions, particularly those which concern the senses of touch and taste. It is selfless "self-preservation." Wherever forces of self-will or self-preservation, self-assertion, or self-fulfillment have the potential to destroy the structure of a person's inner being, the disciplined practice of this virtue enters into play.[40]

Inner-Order includes the subsidiary virtues of simplicity, humility, and self-control which facilitate the practice of effective leadership. Among the marks of greatness often seen in leaders is the virtue of simplicity. Fame and power do not inflate the ego of a leader who practices this virtue. Simplicity is allowing other people to know you accurately--you are what you seem. A leader exhibiting simplicity assures that their ordinary ways of living (i. e., speech, dress, behavior) are consistent with their actual motives and appropriate to the given situation.

Related to simplicity is humility--seeing ourselves as <u>we</u> really are; nothing more, nothing less. The foundation of humility is the recognition of the enormous "gap" which exists between the Creator and myself, between "what I am" and "what I ought to be." Truly humble leaders do not "put on airs" because they realize it is not what a person has that counts but <u>what a person is</u>.

The third subsidiary, self-control, has been called "the essence of character" because its formation or growth requires great effort. Character is formed by a variety of small circumstances, more or less under the regulation of the individual concerned. Every action, thought and feeling contributes something to it, good or bad. Progress in character formation requires the exercise of constant self-control. Self-control enables leaders to control themselves in a fitting manner in any circumstances and makes possible a secure and intelligent <u>self-respect</u> leading to a true and unbiased <u>respect for others</u>.

78

*This much I think I do know
--that a society so riven that
the spirit of moderation
is gone, no court CAN save;
that a society where
that spirit flourishes,
no court NEED save;
that a society which evades
its responsibility by thrusting
upon the courts the nurture
of that spirit, that spirit
in the end will perish.*

**--Learned Hand (1872-1961)--**
*The Contribution of an Independent Judiciary
to Civilization, 1942*

# Reflections on Inner-Order

Inner-Order is vital because it embodies Moderation which is one of the basic qualities of character. And we believe a leader's character DOES make a difference in their effectiveness in leading others. The faculty of inner-order is the ability to practice self-control to keep all activities, influences, and desires, within reasonable limits. It is arguably the most dynamic virtue necessary for **Formative Leadership**.

A leader who has decided to activate the virtues through practical wisdom, tested virtuous behavior through courageous practices, and who considers the rights of others, in justice, also needs to practice this virtue; to seek inner-order through the moderation of substances, emotions, and passions. The exercise of this virtue of self-restraint develops the discipline of self-control which is essential to the development of character.

 History and literature are replete with examples of "good leaders" who have lost their inner-order through immoderate behavior--always with disastrous consequences. Alexander the Great, at the young age of 33, drank himself to a stupor, contracted typhoid fever, and died while celebrating his great victories.

Melville's Captain Ahab in *Moby Dick* pursued the great white whale with such megalomaniacal determination it led to his death and that of his crew. David, the great King of Israel, desired Bathsheba (the wife of his captain, Uriah) so much that he got Uriah killed to make Bathsheba his wife. King David's desire for "self-satisfaction" destroyed the integrity of his inner being.

To neglect the restraint of bodily passions in our relationships destroys the inner will, and makes it difficult, if not impossible to practice the other virtues of wisdom, courage, and justice as well as the subsidiary virtues of each, which truly empower the leader within. It may help to develop a mental model of inner-order as physical exercise, for indeed it inwardly "exercises" the will.

The neglect of physical exercise on the body becomes obvious over time: the body becomes out of shape, overweight, exhibits lack of strength, muscles atrophy, poor circulation develops, and there is an overall indication of health deterioration. In the same way, the abandonment or neglect of self-restraint on the senses may also lead over time to alcoholism, drug addiction, infidelity, gluttony, avarice, disreputable activities, and/or simply laziness; the overall deterioration of inner health, or strength of character.

The exercise of inner-order, similar to physical exercise, keeps the will, character, and the leader's reputation in excellent shape. Not only is good character, like muscle tone, maintained, but the leader has the inner harmony to practice all of the other virtues. No one needs to be reminded of the benefits of keeping physically fit. In the short term, it can make you feel better; in the long term, you could live longer. So, just as moderation of substances leads to good physical health, inner-order leads to a healthy character and peak leadership performance. All leaders need to practice inner-order because of their heavy responsibilities, ability to influence others due to their position, and the need to make good decisions.

The practice of Inner-Order as Moderation applies to our emotions as well as our passions. Leaders ought not let emotions "rule the day." Effective leaders do not base their actions or decisions on feelings alone because feelings can and often do change. And they do not let any one emotion, be it anger, guilt, greed, love, fear or hate tip their inner balance. For some of us emotions may be harder than substances to control, and yet the balance of both calls for the practice of inner-order. The moderation of the emotions is a daily task of balancing the appropriateness of emotional responses to the presenting person, situation, or circumstances at hand.

The practice of the three other essential virtues of Wisdom, Courage, and Justice sets the "standards" of Inner-Order--our "Golden Mean." Right reason may be clouded by our emotional response to a particular person, place or thing. We are unable to act with justice and give others their due if emotions become obstacles to acknowledging the rights of others and exercising virtuous behavior. Our personal desires may have accompanying emotions based on power, position, or possessions and these tainted emotions may weaken or distort our inner selves, so that true practice of wisdom, courage, and justice is not realized. Without wisdom to inform our standards, we may mistake immoderate emotions for courageous endurance or just behavior.

Inner-Order as Moderation can only be acquired through the practice of self-discipline. Through this practice, the will is strengthened to respond to the leader's own personal power of the other virtues which "radiate from within." This virtue is only achieved by maintaining standards of behavior and desire which "illuminate" inner, and "reflect" outer, order. **Formative Leadership** measures these standards in terms of the results achieved. Before one can lead others effectively, one must be able to lead oneself!

*He who exercises government [direction] by means of his virtue may be compared to the north polar star, which keeps its place and all the stars turn towards it.*

**--Confucius--**

*. . . For the duty of a temperate man is not to follow or to avoid what he ought not, but what he ought, whether things or men or pleasures or pains, and patiently to endure when he ought; and therefore, Callicles, the temperate man, being as we have described, also just and courageous and holy, cannot be other than a perfectly good man, nor can the good man do otherwise than well and perfectly whatever he does; and he who does well must of necessity be happy and blessed.*

**--Plato--**

# Exercises in Inner-Order:
## Knowledge/Attitudes/Skills/Relationships

1. Investigate some strategies (e. g., the movie *Ghandi*, Deborah Tannen's book *You Just Don't Understand*, etc.)[41] for overcoming harmful habits you may have regarding the virtue of Inner-Order as Moderation or its three subsidiaries--simplicity, humility, self-control. Record in your journal lessons learned and a plan of action for improvement.

2. Try not to think of self-control as "giving up" something you like. No one wants to lose anything! Instead, transform your attitude by measuring success in positive terms (i. e., instead of setting a goal not to loose your temper under stress, say "I will treat others as I would like to be treated--with respect and consideration"). This will help your mind-set in terms of establishing positive self-talk. Remember self-control enables a leader to progress in character formation.

3. Identify three vices or irrational emotional responses which keep you from practicing inner-order. Work on eliminating these vices or responses by practicing the opposing virtues. Record daily how these new practices are progressing.

# Through virtue lies the one and only road to a life of peace.

**---Juvenal--**

## The Virtue-Quest™ . . .

is a fun exercise which takes about 6 to 10 minutes to complete. It is a review of what the book has covered so far and prepares you for applying the principles in **Part 3: Praxis.**

## The Quest begins here:

You have chosen to embark on a mission of self-discovery. You are attempting to discover the forgotten wisdom of an ancient cultural heritage--namely, your own! You are actually re-discovering that which former generations knew as the time-tested and true methods of developing the knowledge, attitudes, skills, and relationships necessary for **Formative Leadership**.

Use your newfound power of knowledge to review how well you remember the "key" concepts. If you successfully complete this "test," you know you will be ready to move to the next level of the journey.

Answer each question and carefully follow the directions given at the end of each chosen response. Remember: In order to give directions to others, you ought to be able to follow directions yourself. Always keep "first things first," as Covey said;

### so, start at #1!

#1.    The word "virtue" comes from the Latin "virtus," meaning, in essence, "power."

TRUE, Virtus means Power  (Go to #7)

FALSE, Virtus does not mean Power  (Go to #10)

#2.    Try again.  Gratitude is a subsidiary virtue of Justice (giving others their due).  By gratitude, we mean being sincere in our thankfulness to others for their contributions.  In order to inspire others to follow, a leader must be grateful, recognizing others' accomplishments.  Now be grateful for the chance to go back to #4 and try again!

#3.    Who said, "Excellence is a habit, not an act?"

PLATO ...            (Go to #6)

ARISTOTLE ...      (Go to #9)

SOCRATES ...       (Go to #12)

#4.    Which of the following virtues is a subsidiary virtue of Wisdom?

GRATITUDE ...          (Go to #2)

DISCERNMENT ...        (Go to #8)

SELF-CONTROL ...       (Go to #11)

#5.    The word "CARDINAL," as in 4 Cardinal Virtues, comes from the Latin "Cardo" meaning "hinge."

TRUE,  Cardo means hinge in Latin.  (Go to #21)

FALSE, Cardo does <u>not</u> mean hinge.  (Go to #13)

#6.    Plato said many wise things.  Unfortunately, he never said that excellence is a habit, not an act.  If you are interested in discovering where Plato said some of <u>his</u> wise things, go to #17; then go back to #3, and try again!

#7.    Right, Virtus is Latin for Power!  On with *The Quest*, go to #4.

#8.    You have discerned correctly!  Discernment is a subsidiary virtue of Wisdom.  It is the ability to recognize the various factors which influence feelings and behaviors, and be able to make good leadership decisions based on these factors and the impact of those decisions on others.  You're now ready to go to #3.

#9.    You really know your Greek philosophers!  Aristotle did say that "excellence is a habit, not an act."  He meant that one isolated act doesn't cut it.  One must constantly work at it to develop the <u>habit</u> of each virtue.  Now, continue *The Quest*.  On to #14.

#10.    Try again. "Virtus" does indeed mean "power" in Latin. That is why we maintain that the power to achieve peak leadership performance comes from the practice of the 4 essential virtues! Be of good cheer! *The Quest* has only just begun. Use the power of your new knowledge to start again.
Go back to #1.


#11.    Self-control is not a subsidiary of Wisdom. Self-control is a subsidiary of Courage because true control, or the ability to bear present difficulties calmly for the sake of a higher good, takes great courage and strength. Try again!
Go back to #4.


#12    No, Socrates just <u>wished</u> he had said that excellence is a habit, not an act. You've gotten your Greeks garbled. With a little effort, you can sort them out! The prize at the end of the quest is worth the trial. Give it another try!
Go back to #3.


#13.    Uh oh, "cardo" does indeed mean "hinge." Next you'll be trying to convince us that they are called the "Cardinal Virtues" because a little redbird told you so! Attention to detail helps develop the habit of practicing the virtues. You may now proceed.
Go to #18.

#14.  Which of the Cardinal Virtues helps us to decide to activate all the other virtues in our efforts to empower the leader within?

COURAGE?  (Go to #19)

WISDOM?  (Go to #20)

INNER-ORDER?  (Go to #24)


#15.  Inner-Order as Moderation is the "Golden Mean" between excess (too much of a good thing) and defect (not enough of a good thing).  The effective leader seeks inner-order by the appropriate use of "things" in moderation.  Total abstinence from alcohol is not REQUIRED to be "moderate," by definition of the word.  However, a good leader will remember that one leads best by example.
Go to #28.


#16.  This is a "chicken-or-the-egg" question.  Piety, not covered in this book, is one of the subsidiary virtues of Justice (giving the Creator proper due).  One can possess the human virtues without being overtly religious; but it is highly unlikely that someone who disdains positive spiritual realities will practice the human virtues.  And, this person will certainly not be able to practice the spiritual virtues of FAITH, HOPE, and CHARITY--a subject which you will find in another book altogether!
Go to #29.

#17.	Plato was the student of Socrates and the teacher of Aristotle. In his book *Republic*, he refers to the "Philosopher King" as the perfect example of a virtuous leader. You should "give it a read" when you get finished with *The Quest*.
Now go back to #3!

#18.	Inner-Order as Moderation means that a person should abstain totally from alcohol in order to keep oneself virtuous.
TRUE? (Go to #26)		FALSE? (Go to #15)

#19.	Courage gives us the strength and tenacity to live the other virtues. We must use a different virtue to decide to live the virtues. Have Courage, do not let this minor setback keep you from completing *The Quest*! Persevere!
Go back to #14.

#20.	A Wise choice! Wisdom is the virtue which helps us to gather information, assess that information in the light of objective standards and weigh the favorable and not-so-favorable consequences of our decisions. Well done, proceed (backward) to #5.

#21.	You must be a Latin scholar! "Cardo" means "hinge" in English. We call them the four Cardinal Virtues because they are "hinges" upon which "swing the gates of life." These four essential virtues are the "sine qua non" of **Formative Leadership**! Go to #18.

#22. It is a wonder that you have come this far and still do not believe. Try to suspend judgement. Re-read the first part of this book and give it some serious thought. We hope, one day, you will see the wisdom of the virtues. First, please read #30.

#23. Right you are! One does not have to be overtly religious. But don't be too smug. You have a couple more tasks before completing *The Quest*. Read #16 thoroughly before proceeding to the final stop #29.

#24. Guess again. This time try harder! Please go back 10 steps to #14.

#25. *The Quest* is almost history, but you are on your way to truly empowering the leader within! You are almost ready to complete the rest of this book and actually apply these principles in your daily life. Well done! Now, on to the last one, #30.

#26. Inner-Order as Moderation does not REQUIRE total abstinence from alcohol. It is the Cardinal Virtue of self-restraint; avoiding both excess and defect in our undertakings as a leader. It is the "temperate zone" between the steamy tropics and the frozen tundra; the happy medium between too much and too little of a good thing. You're almost finished, go to #28.

#27. Answer: Jesus of Nazareth said it and the virtue is Humility--a necessity for any leader who is truly empowered from within to serve others.

#28. In order to be virtuous, one must be religious.

YES, virtue flows from strong religious convictions. Go to #16.

NO, one doesn't need to be overtly "religious" to be virtuous.
Go to #23.

#29. You have now reached the penultimate step on *The Quest* but you are not finished yet. Consider this: To truly empower the leader within, does character really matter?

YES, character matters and practicing the human virtues will help a person achieve peak leadership performance.
Go to #25.

NO, for a leader, only one thing really matters is results--the "bottom line!"
Go to #22.

#30.    This part of *The Quest* is finished. But you are far from finished in applying the virtues to daily life. **Formative Leadership** is a life-long learning experience of trial and error; of picking yourself up from defeat and pressing on to victory. You will find that you must begin and begin again! Ultimately, it doesn't matter how well you did on *The Quest*. What we <u>know</u> doesn't necessarily change our <u>behavior,</u> unless we first change our <u>attitude</u>. Before you continue with your life's journey, do you know what "Servant Leader" said "He who would be first among you, must become last" and what subsidiary virtue of Wisdom he was recommending? If not, before you go <u>read #27</u>!

By the way, if you were looking for a "prize" at the end of *The Quest*, then you have indeed found one, for, as the ancient saying goes:

## *Virtue is its own reward.*

## *Officu fructus sit ipsum officium.*

**--Cicero--**

# PART THREE: PRAXIS

*Consider your origin;
you were born not to live
like brutes, but to follow
virtue and knowledge.*

--Dante Alighieri--

# Formative Leadership as Personal Power: Virtue-in-Action

**Formative Leadership as Personal Power**--empowering the leader within--is **Virtue-in-Action**. Remember, <u>action follows being</u>! Therefore, **Formative Leadership** is achieved by the things we choose to do! You have been given the four "golden" keys. But, now you must choose to use them in order to open the repositories containing the knowledge, attitudes, and skills which will ensure you the power to achieve peak leadership performance. You must take <u>action</u> in order to acquire the necessary character-building **habits** which enable you to activate this power wisely in any situation. This section presents some ideas to enable you to put <u>virtue into action</u>.

## Formative Leadership From Vision to Reality
## --A 3 Step Process--

We all really are creatures of habit! By habit, we mean an acquired facility, or ease, in doing things without thought. Life is greatly a matter of habits--like dressing, reading, writing, cycling, and such.

How do you acquire any habit then? <u>They are acquired by the frequent repetition of the same act.</u> Practice makes perfect! That is an old truism which affects life seriously. You did have to learn to crawl before you could walk. And, you probably fell off of your bicycle many times before you mastered the art of cycling.

Another axiom that must be understood is this: _a habit makes an act easy to do but does not force us to do that act_! What is meant by this? Consider the following example.

You do not ride a bicycle because the habit of cycling forces you to do so, but if you wish to cycle, then the habit makes it easy for you to cycle without any difficulty. After repeated attempts, muscle memory takes over and you do not even have to think about how to ride perfectly. But, you still have to decide that you want to ride your bike before actually doing it.

So with all habits; <u>though they give the facility, they cannot force action unless it is willed</u>. This truth has a critical significance in the consideration of developing good habits (virtues).

Virtues often seem such difficult things to acquire; on the other hand, vices (bad habits) are frequently only too easy. How then does a leader get rid of bad habits (vices) and acquire good ones (virtues)?

Take an inflated ego, for example. It usually stems from self-centeredness or conceit, and therefore it is contrary to the subsidiary virtue of inner-order--humility--and probably also to justice as far as others are concerned. It is by continual acts of generosity that this habit is rectified; <u>the only way to eliminate the vice is to practice the opposing virtue</u>. For example, pride may be rectified by acts of modesty; bad-temper by acts of tolerance; laziness by industry. Each vice has an opposing virtue; the acquisition of the virtue will usually end in the elimination of the corresponding vice.

What might be an effective process to follow in order to acquire these character-building habits (virtues) and develop the "muscle memory" in order to empower the leader within?  One must, as Socrates said, "Master thyself," which involves the following simple, yet very powerful, **3 Step Process:**[42]

## STEP 1  Self-Knowledge (Evaluation),
which leads to

## STEP 2  Self-Discipline (Organization),
which next leads to

## STEP 3 Self-Sacrifice (Resolution)
in service to others.

It is our belief that following this **3 Step Process** will enable you to transform your "vision to reality" in your journey to **Formative Leadership.**  It will facilitate your turning the vision of the leader you would like to become into the reality of being that leader--wise/prudent, just, and courageous, with inner-order.

In order to assist you in applying each one of the steps in this process,  we have developed some tools and aids which are presented in the following sections.   They are designed for you to commission yourself in developing the peak leadership performance you desire.

101

*"Would you tell me,*
*please, which way*
*I ought to go from here?*
*That depends a good deal*
*on where you want to go,"*
*said the cat.*
*"I don't much care where*
*--so long as I get somewhere,"*
*Alice added as an explanation.*
*"Oh, you're sure to do that,"*
*said the cat.*
*"If you only walk long enough."*

**--Lewis Carroll--**
*Alice's Adventures in Wonderland, 1865*

# STEP 1 Self-Knowledge (Evaluation)

Knowledge is the beginning of the change process! In STEP 1 of the **3 Step Process**, you can begin to gain <u>Self-Knowledge</u> through an <u>evaluation</u> or assessment of your current situation. You can do this by first reflecting on your present behavior, then completing a personal self-assessment, and measuring the results.

This process will help you to identify any gaps between where you are now and where you want to be in the future and help you determine your *Virtue Quotient.*™ Next, you need to analyze those forces which may help or hinder you in achieving your improvement goals.

## *Virtue-Reality Square*™

The first phase of the evaluation process is to reflect on your present behavior in order to gain an awareness of it. Awareness (knowledge) of reality (being) plays a large role in the effort to will (attitude) the action (behavior) to change.

For example, in learning to bike ride you first became aware that bicycling was a desirable activity that you did not know how to do. Next, you had to desire to ride. And, finally you practiced riding until it became second nature. In other words, you first needed an awareness of your situation before deciding to take some action to change.

The model on the next page, which we call the **Virtue-Reality Square,**™ depicts the relationship between our awareness of our behavior (conscious action) and the acquisition (or competency level) of a specific virtue. This model is designed to be used as an aid in helping you become more aware of your situation (attitudes) before planning how to change your behavior in order to make it more virtuous.

An individual in Square I, goes through life unaware that their behavior is not virtuous in a specific regard (i. e., a person who lacks perseverance and gives up too easily whenever an obstacle is encountered). Usually, to progress to Square II, a Significant Emotional Event happens (e. g., reading a book or attending a seminar on self improvement, or experiencing a change in life--career, life transition, marital status, etc.) and the person now "sees" or gains insight that they have been unaware that they were not virtuous.

Next, with some effort focused on acquiring the needed virtue (i. e., perseverance), the person moves into Square III, in which they are constantly aware that they are practicing the HABITS necessary to form the desired virtue. Finally, after much effort, an individual is "unconsciously competent" or reaches Square IV, in which the virtuous behavior is automatic and performed without awareness.

|  | Unaware of<br>Behavior | Aware of<br>Behavior |
|---|---|---|
| **Not<br>Virtuous** | I | II |
| **Virtuous** | IV | III |

## Virtue-Reality Square™

Square I -- Unaware of the fact you are Not Virtuous
    (have unacknowledged bad habits)

Square II -- Aware you are Not Virtuous
    (practicing bad habits)

Square III-- Aware of your Virtuous behavior
    (practicing good habits)

Square IV--Unaware of Virtuous behavior
    (good habits become second nature)

## *Virtue-Reality Check*™

Human beings are naturally goal oriented. We need an end or an aim toward which our efforts are directed. The scene from *Alice's Adventures in Wonderland* described on page 102 illustrates this point nicely.

If your goal as a leader is to simply get somewhere, anywhere, you can be sure to do that by working long enough and hard enough. But, if you do not know where you are going (what your aim is) you probably will not like it when you get there. If, however, you know your goal is to get to a particular destination for a specific reason, then you need to identify it, see it clearly, and act on it.

How important is goal setting to **Formative Leadership**? *SMI International, Inc..*, a company dedicated to motivating people to their full potential, found that only the "top 3%" of the population usually had written, specific goals and a way to keep score. The next 10% of the people had goals generally in mind, but they were not written nor specific. And the majority, 87%, had no goals beyond making a living or surviving from day to day, usually at only the subsistence level.[43]

The numbers from the *SMI* study would seem to indicate that for a leader who is committed to achieving peak leadership performance, goal setting is important. Visualizing those goals to make them a reality is absolutely essential!

Let us consider an incident out of the life of Florence Chadwick. She was the first woman to swim the English Channel in both directions. Her story illustrates the importance of having clearly visualized goals.

According to an unpublished report of the event, the coast of California was shrouded in fog the morning of the fourth of July, 1952.[44] On Catalina Island, twenty-one miles to the west, 34-year-old Florence Chadwick waded into the water and started swimming toward the coast of California, resolved on being the first woman to accomplish the feat.

The water was numbing cold and the fog was "thicker than pea soup." An estimated millions were viewing the event on television. Several times sharks had to be driven away to protect the solitary swimmer. Florence swam on as the hours slowly passed.

After fifteen hours of swimming, anesthetized by the "bone-chilling" cold, she requested to be taken out of the water. Her mother and personal trainer told Florence that land was near and urged her not to quit. But when Florence looked toward the California coast, all she could see was the impenetrable fog. So, at fifteen hours and fifty-five minutes into the swim she was taken out of the water.

The impact of failure set in some hours later. She exclaimed to a reporter, "Look, I'm not excusing myself. But if I could have <u>seen</u> land, I might have made it."

Florence had quit swimming only one-half mile from the coast of California! Upon reflection she realized that she had been defeated neither by fatigue nor cold. But, the fog solely had been her nemesis--it had "obscured her goal . . . it had blinded her reason, her eyes, her heart."

This was the only instance Florence Chadwick ever abandoned a goal--but, not for long. Two months later she swam the same channel. The fog again was "thicker than pea soup"--obscuring her vision anew. This time, however, she swam with her "faith intact"--somewhere beyond that impenetrable fog was land. This time Florence Chadwick became the first woman to swim the Catalina Channel, and while she was at it, she trounced the man's record by over two hours!

What follows next is the second tool to assist you in completing the second phase of STEP 1, Self-Knowledge (evaluation). It is the *Virtue-Reality Check*™, which you can use to help in identifying and measuring any gaps in your current leadership character to determine your *Virtue Quotient*™. The results of this survey will serve as important input to facilitate you in clearly visualizing your goals in order to develop a plan of action for improvement.

*For lack of training, they lacked knowledge.*
*For lack of knowledge, they lacked confidence.*
*For lack of confidence, they lacked victory.*

**--Gaius Julius Caesar (100 to 44 B.C.)--**

## *Virtue-Reality Check*™

*Please read carefully and answer these questions honestly.
Place the <u>NUMBER</u> of the response you most agree with
next to each statement below:*

| --1-- | --2-- | --3-- | --4-- | --5-- | --6-- |
|---|---|---|---|---|---|
| Strongly Disagree | Disagree | Mildly Disagre | Mildly Agree | Agree | Strongly Agree |

___A.    When events get tough in life, I am strong enough to see things through adversity.

___B.    I always give others their due whether I feel like it or not.

___C.    My life is one of total inner order.

___D.    I usually settle for "good enough," for things I know which are "not quite right."

___E.    The truth of the matter is, I find it difficult to overlook pettiness, insult, or injury which has been caused by others.

___F.    I'm a "good winner"-- I'm "gentle" to my opponents in victory.

___G.    I am passionate about ensuring that true justice be done for all--even when things go against my personal preferences.

___H.    It is better to tell a "white lie" every once in a while than to tell somebody what you really think.

___I.    My motto is "Everything in moderation!"

___J.    I think of myself as a very prudent person who makes "wise" decisions.

--1--     --2--     --3--     --4--     --5--     --6--
Strongly Disagree I Disagree I Mildly Disagre I Mildly Agree I Agree I Strongly Agree

___K.    I do not believe that "gentleness" is a sign of weakness.

___L.    I am one of the most responsible people I know.

___M.    I have a highly developed sense of what is fair and I am always equitable in my dealings with others.

___N.    So-called "discernment" is really an excuse for inability to think on your feet.

___O.    I try to see myself as I really am. Nothing more, nothing less!

___P.    I always take proper precaution. I am never reckless or so cautious that I fail to respond either appropriately or in a timely manner.

___Q.    I am always quick to show gratitude toward others.

___R.    My life is the picture of perfect orderliness.

___S.    I believe "insight" is one of my strongest virtues.

___T.    I value my right-reasoning as one of my most notable traits.

## *Virtue-Reality Wheel*™
### *...Plotting & Interpreting Your Score*

Chart your item responses to the *Virtue-Reality Check*™ on the *Virtue-Reality Wheel* ™ below. NOTE: "Strongly Agree" = "6" on the spoke of the *Wheel* which corresponds to the specific item "A" through "T" in question. "Agree" = "5"; "Mildly Agree" = "4"; "Mildly Disagree" = "3"; "Disagree" = "2"; "Strongly Disagree" = "1". Also note that items "E," "H," "K," and "N" have a reversed order of lowest to highest. Stick to the same numerical values noted above, which will simply reverse the direction from low to high for those four items only.

After you have transferred your responses to the *Wheel*, you can begin to assess your self-reported degree of each of the four virtues:

> Items J, N, P, S, and T will indicate your "Wisdom quotient."
> Items B, G, H, M, and Q indicate your "Justice quotient."
> Items C, D, I, O, and R indicate your "Inner-Order quotient."
> Items A, E, F, K, and L indicate your "Courage quotient."

Look for gaps. The closer your scores are to the outer ring, the higher your self-assessed degree of that particular virtue. By "connecting the dots," or connecting the scores on each spoke with straight lines, you can begin to see patterns in the data for each virtue. Use this information for beginning an improvement plan of action.

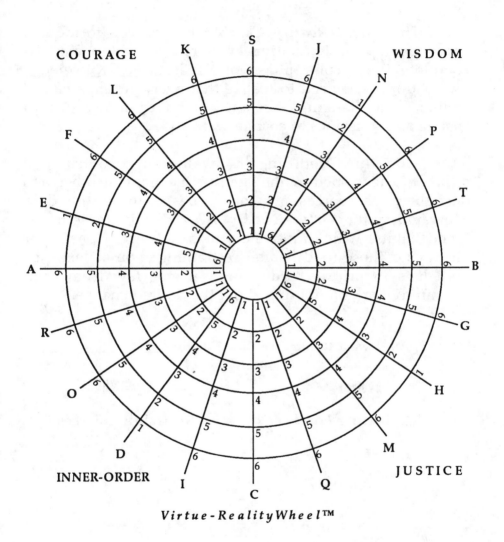

*Virtue-RealityWheel*™

113

## *Force Field Analysis*

The *Virtue-Reality Check*™ helped you to identify any gaps in your **Formative Leadership** development. To complete the second phase of STEP 1, <u>Self-Knowledge</u> (evaluation), you need to realize that every "change effort" results from changing a balance of forces--motivation to change and resistance to change.

This third tool in the evaluation process is a technique, developed by the late Kurt Lewin, which helps to describe those forces at work. Based upon the data generated by the *Virtue-Reality Wheel*™ , list those forces (good habits) which motivate you to acquire a particular virtue and those (bad habits) restraining you. Next, put both lists in priority order and select a few from each column to work on to bring about the desired change.

SITUATION--I want to improve the virtue of:_____

**Motivating Forces**             **Restraining Forces**

1.                        1.

2.                        2.

3.                        3.

4.                        4.

# *Success is the progressive realization of predetermined, worthwhile goals, stabilized with balance and purified by belief.*

**--Glenn Bland[45]--**

## STEP 2  Self-Discipline (Organization)

The formula for developing strong character is the practice of self-discipline.  Remember the 5 P's of business-- Prior Planning Prevents Poor Performance.  To help accomplish STEP 2, Self-Discipline, you will need to develop an action plan.  The action plan is an organization method designed to help you reach your goals.

Remember Murphy's Law:  "whatever can go wrong usually will," and "Murphy was an optimist"; so, keep your plan flexible!  You will need to make a commitment to do those things which you need to do in order to acquire each new habit you desire.  To do this, you will need to envision where you want to be, write a personal mission statement, set worthwhile goals, and generate specific activities to help you get there.

Once a decision has been made, you need to establish your goals and form a plan to help take the action to achieve them.  Without an action plan and commitment to accomplish them, your goals would be merely dreams.

**Formative Leadership**--empowering the leader within--is the goal.  The "golden" keys--the four essential human virtues and their particular subsidiary virtues--are the means.  Developing virtuous habits are the ways.

What follows next are the details to help you develop a **Plan of Action and Commitment Timetable**. Your personal **P.A.C.T.** to accomplish your goals.

116

## *Virtue-P.A.C.T.*™
## . . . Plan of Action & Commitment Timetable

**VIRTUE:** _____

(NOTE: To determine which Key or Subsidiary virtue needs most
attention, refer back to the *Virtue-Reality Wheel*™ *virtue quotients.*
Remember, "accentuate the positive, eliminate the negative.")

**PERSONAL MISSION STATEMENT** [Write a statement which
focuses on what you want to be (character) and to do (achievements
and/or contributions ) for the virtue you are developing.]
Complete the following statement:

I want to be _____

_____

so that I can _____

_____

**GOALS** (They should be S.M.A.R.T.--Specific, Measurable, Attainable,
Realistic, and Tangible/Timely for each area of improvement.)

**Short Term Goals, 6 Months-1 Year:** _____

_____

_____

**Mid-Term Goals, 3-5 Years:** _____

_____

**CHANGE STRATEGY** (In order from easiest to hardest to do, list specific actions you will take to accomplish the changes/reach the goals you desire.):

| Specific Actions | Start Date | End Date |
|---|---|---|
| 1. _____ | _____ | _____ |
| 2. _____ | _____ | _____ |
| 3. _____ | _____ | _____ |
| 4. _____ | _____ | _____ |

**Visualization** (You need to form a clear mental image of each goal as though it had already been actualized.)
Imagine yourself in a hot-air balloon looking down on yourself 5 years from now; picture a "perfect" environment.
What are you doing? Where are you? What is happening around you?:

_____

_____

**Affirmation** (Write a sentence stating a specific reality about your future self, improvement, benefits of the change, etc., as though the reality were already factual.) Finish this statement:
"As a result of positive action, I am beginning to realize . . .

_____

_____

118

*When the best leader's work is done the people say, "We did it ourselves."*

--Lao-Tzu (c. 604 B. C.)[46]--

## STEP 3 Self-Sacrifice (Resolution)

This is the moment of truth! Now is the time for action. The secret of self-disciplined character lies in the repetition of worthy acts--sometimes requiring heroic effort in the ordinary things.

So, STEP 3, <u>Self-Sacrifice</u> (Resolution), will require that you seek opportunities to perform frequent repetition of the acts exercising the virtue; to try and never make any exceptions to the rule, until the virtue is acquired and you are ready to move on to the next area of improvement. This step is not easy, and you can expect many lapses; make the resolve to <u>begin and begin again</u>. Perseverance will win in the end, "good Lord willing, and the creek don't rise!"

## *Measuring Progress--Vision to Reality*

You have made a resolve to empower the leader within yourself by acquiring the character-building habits (virtues) necessary to do so. But how will you measure results?

If you don't <u>inspect</u> what you <u>expect</u>, you probably will not get what you expect. A simple, but effective method, is to keep a daily log recording your activities, a la old Ben Franklin (i. e., using a **virtue checklist**, place hatch marks ⊤⊦⊦⊦ next to the virtue practiced, one for each act performed). Periodic review will help you to see how you have made measurable improvement in performance, and help you to determine where you need further work.

| Days on which specific activities conducted to improve virtue. | | | | | | | |
|---|---|---|---|---|---|---|---|
| Virtues: | SUN. | MON. | TUE. | WED. | THR. | FRI. | SAT. |
| WISDOM | | | | | | | |
| Insight | | | | | | | |
| Discernment | | | | | | | |
| Decision-Making | | | | | | | |
| COURAGE | | | | | | | |
| Risk-Taking | | | | | | | |
| Responsibility | | | | | | | |
| Self-Sacrifice | | | | | | | |
| JUSTICE | | | | | | | |
| Fairness | | | | | | | |
| Honesty | | | | | | | |
| Gratitude | | | | | | | |
| INNER-ORDER | | | | | | | |
| Simplicity | | | | | | | |
| Humility | | | | | | | |
| Self-Control | | | | | | | |

# *Formative Leadership--Epilogue*

It is wise to remember that **Formative Leadership**--empowering the leader within--is a journey, NOT a destination. And the four essential virtues (Wisdom, Justice, Courage, and Inner-Order) are the "golden" keys and the foundation we need to embark upon the journey.

Peter Kreeft, in *Back to Virtue*, probably summed it up most succinctly:

> These four cardinal virtues are not the only virtues, but they are the *cardes*, the "hinges," on which all the other virtues turn. They are the necessary foundation and precondition for all others. If a person is not courageous, for instance, (that person) will not overcome the difficulties inherent in the practice of any virtue. If (that person) is not wise, (they) will not understand what (they are) doing, and (their) virtue will sink to the level of blind animal instinct.
>
> There are many more virtues than these--there is always more--for "there are more things in heaven and earth than are dreamt of in your philosophy." But never less.

> This is the foundation. This must be built, or rebuilt, first . . . . If we are to rebuild our civilization, of if we are to build a new one, we need to build on foundations whose posts reach down into our own being, at least . . .
> (p. 68).[47]

You are already making progress on your journey to empower the leader within. You are reading this book and understanding the significance of where real power originates--from character formation. You are evaluating your knowledge, organizing your behavior to gain control of your actions, and resolving gaps in your behavior evidenced through our service to others.

You are also envisioning a different self, a more powerful leader, a respected colleague and friend to many, a champion of justice to all. You are setting goals to achieve that vision through your P.A.C.T. with yourself. But most importantly, you are creating new hope for the future. You have come to believe that character DOES matter, and your actions will give meaning to your words.

In a world where women and men practice wisdom in decision-making, have the courage to act on their ethical beliefs, treat others with dignity through true justice, and monitor the balance and demonstration of their own inner-order, that is a world of great leaders, great expectations, and great accomplishments. It is a vision that we bring to reality by **Formative Leadership**--empowering the leader within through the practice of the four essential virtues.

# End Notes

1. Maxwell, J. C. *Leadership 101: Inspirational Quotes & Insights for Leaders.* Oklahoma: Honor Books, 1994.

2. Bennis, W., and Nanus, B. *Leaders: The Strategies for Taking Charge.* New York: Harper & Row, 1985.

3. Bennis and Nanus, *Leaders. . .*

4. Deming, W. E. *Out of the Crisis*, 1986, see Chapter 8, and *The New Economics for Industry, Government, Education*, 1993, see Chapter 5-- Cambridge, MA: MIT Center for Advanced Engineering Study; Juran, J. M. *Juran on Leadership for Quality: An Executive Handbook.* New York: The Free Press, 1989; and *Malcolm Baldrige National Quality Award 1995 Award Criteria.* American Society of Quality Control: "The Leadership category examines executives' *personal* leadership and involvement in creating and sustaining . . .*clear values* and expectations. . . ."

5. Greenberg, J. *Organizational Behavior: The State of the Science.* New Jersey: Lawrence Exlbaum Associates, Publishers, 1994.

6. Maxwell, *Leadership 101. . .*

7. *Hewlett-Packhard's success built on concern for people.* The Baltimore Sun, 1995, p. 4E.

8. Pfeiffer, R. (Ed.) *Theories & Models in Applied Behavioral Science (Vol. 3), Management/Leadership.* San Diego: Pfeiffer & Company, 1991, pp. 215-218.

9. Greenberg, *Organizational Behavior. . .*

10. Stogdill, R. M. *Handbook of Leadership: A Survey of Theory and Research.* New York: Free Press, 1974.

11. Burns, J. M. *Leadership.* New York: Harper & Row, 1978.

12. Covey, S. R. *Principle-Centered Leadership*. New York: Fireside, 1991.

13. Cited in McDermott, R. E., Mikulak, R. J., and Beauregard, M. R. *Employee Driven Quality*. New York: Quality Resources, 1993, p. 54.

14. Bass, B. M. *Stogdill's Handbook of Leadership*. New York: The Free Press, 1981; Block, P. *The Empowered Manager*. San Francisco: Jossey-Bass, 1987; Burns, *Leadership. . .*; and Maslow, A. H. *Motivation and Personality (2nd. ed.)*. New York: Harper & Row, 1970.

15. Burns, *Leadership. . .*

16. Maxwell, *Leadership 101. . .*

17. Covey, S. R. *The 7 Habits of Highly Effective People.: Restoring the Character Ethic*. New York: Fireside, 1990.

18. Much of the discussion on character draws upon the theoretical framework delineated in *Character Guidance Topics* issued by the Departments of the Army and Air Force, 1951, Series I-VI.

19. Maxwell, *Leadership 101. . .*

20. Shula, D. and Blanchard, K. *Everyone's A Coach*. New York: Harper Business, 1995.

21. Woodward, K. L. *What is Virtue?* NEWSWEEK, June 13, 1994, pp. 38-39.

22. Isaacs, D. *Character Building*. County Dublin: Four Courts Press (translation), 1993, p. 13.

23. Covey, *Principle-Centered Leadership. . .*

24. Kreeft, P. *Back to Virtue*. San Francisco: Ignatius Press, 1992. Kreeft listed the Four Cardinal Virtues as: wisdom (prudence) as understanding, courage (fortitude) as nonphysical, moderation (temperance) vs. materialism, and justice as harmony.

125

25. Maxwell, *Leadership 101. . .*

26. Pieper, J. *The Four Cardinal Virtues.* Indiana: University of Notre Dame Press, 1966.

27. Kreeft, in *Back to Virtue. . .* stated: ". . . these new values [virtues] fit the new psychology . . .: moderation . . . for the id, for animal desires; courage . . . for the ego, or will; and wisdom . . . for the superego, or conscience, or mind. Our new values fit our nature. Justice is the harmony or integration or adjustment . . . of all the different parts . . . . From Plato to Freud, common sense, philosophy, and psychology have found themselves talking about some version of this <u>tripartite-soul</u> idea [memory, understanding, will] with virtue as its health. This is *natural*, like a heavy body falling to its natural place . . ." (pp. 62-63).

28. Bettger, F. *How I Raised Myself From Failure to Success in Selling.* New York: Cornerstone Library, 1982 (Reprint); and Roberts, H. V. and Sergesketter, B. F. *Quality is Personal.* New York: The Free Press, 1993.

29. Maxwell, *Leadership 101. . .*

30. Bennett, W. *Positive Employee Practices Institute Conference.* Atlanta, GA, 1995.

31. Woodward, *What is Virtue?. . .*

32. Bennis and Nanus, *Leaders. . .*

33. Covey, *Principle-Centered Leadership. . .*; and Kouzes, J. M., and Posner, B. Z. *The Leadership Challenge.* San Francisco: Jossey-Bass Publishers, 1987.

34. Kennedy, J. F. *Profiles in Courage.* New York: Pocket Books, Inc., 1960; and Keller, H. A. *The Story of My Life.* New York: Bantam Books, 1990.

35. Pieper, *The Four Cardinal Virtues. . .*

36. Shula and Blanchard, *Everyone's A Coach. . .*

37. *Character Guidance Topics.. . .*

38. Maxwell, *Leadership 101. . .*

39. Bennett, W. *The Book of Virtues.* New York: Simon & Schuster, 1993.

40. Pieper, *The Four Cardinal Virtues. . .*

41. *Ghandi,* the movie, available on video tape; and Tannen, D. *You Just Don't Understand Me.* New York: Ballantine Books, 1990.

42. Isaacs, *Character Building.. . .* We are indebted to Isaacs for first presenting this framework: "To develop the different aspects of our inner core and personality (and, as a result, our personal freedom), first of all one needs to know oneself. We need to know each person's qualities in order to be able to discover the best way for him to improve and develop. Development involves three stages (1) self-knowledge, leading to (2) self-discipline leading to (3) self-surrender i.e. the service of others. This over-all development is achieved through growth in human virtues. . . . Society clearly needs these virtues to develop in each of its members. . . . A virtue may be developed in relation to two aspects: the intensity with which it is practiced and the rightness of the motivation underlying its practice. In society, generally, the interest shown in virtues is motivated by achieving better performance. That is, people tend to develop a series of human virtues because they need to perform better. . . ." (p. 7)

43. *Measurable Improvement in Performance.* Texas: SMI International, Inc., 1980.

44. *The Importance of Visualization,* unpublished report, anon.

45. Bland, G. *Success!* Illinois: Living Books, 1983.

46. Maxwell, *Leadership 101. . .*

47. Kreeft, *Back to Virtue. . .*

# About the Center for Formative Leadership

*The Center for Formative Leadership* is dedicated to "<u>empowering the leader within</u>" people to "<u>achieve peak leadership performance</u>" at work, at home, or in any social situation. *The Center's* programs and services provide a wide variety of resources for leaders in business, government, and educational organizations, as well as for individuals and families, including: training opportunities such as seminars, a small group workshop series, and leadership retreats, as well as a newsletter, books, and other customized resources designed to increase your inner ability to lead others for positive results.

**FOR MORE INFORMATION ON OUR SERVICES,**

**OR TO ORDER MORE COPIES OF**

*EMPOWERING THE LEADER WITHIN. . .*

# CALL:

**The Center for Formative Leadership**

# 410-747-0003

**24 Hour Recorded Message Gives Complete Details!**